50 SPACE MISSIONS THAT CHANGED THE WORLD

JOHN A. READ

Formac Publishing Company Limited
Halifax

A very special thanks to space historians Chris Gainor (past president of the Royal Astronomical Society of Canada and author of Arrows to the Moon) *and Randy Attwood (former Executive Director of the The Royal Astronomical Society of Canada, journalist and Canadian Space Agency photographer).*

Formac Publishing Company Limited and Stellar Publishing recognize the support of the Province of Nova Scotia through the Department of Communities, Culture and Heritage. We are pleased to work in partnership with the Province of Nova Scotia to develop and promote our cultural resources for all Nova Scotians. We acknowledge the support of the Canada Council for the Arts, which last year invested $153 million to bring the arts to Canadians throughout the country. This project has been made possible in part by the Government of Canada.

Cover Design: Tyler Cleroux
Cover photos: Shutterstock and NASA

Library and Archives Canada Cataloguing in Publication

Title: 50 space missions that changed the world / John A. Read.
Other titles: Fifty space missions that changed the world
Names: Read, John A., author.
Description: Includes bibliographical references.
Identifiers: Canadiana 20200206818 | ISBN 9781459506268 (hardcover)
Subjects: LCSH: Manned space flight—History. | LCSH: Outer space—
    Exploration—History.
Classification: LCC TL788.5 .R43 2020 | DDC 629.4/1—dc23

Published by:
Formac Publishing
Company Limited
5502 Atlantic Street
Halifax, NS, Canada
B3H 1G4
www.formac.ca

Distributed in
Canada by:
Formac Lorimer Books
5502 Atlantic Street
Halifax, NS, Canada
B3H 1G4

Distributed in the US by:
Lerner Publisher Services
1251 Washington Ave. N.
Minneapolis, MN, USA
55401
www.lernerbooks.com

Printed and bound in Korea.
Manufactured by We Sp. Co., Ltd
Job #200824

TABLE OF CONTENTS

Changing the World

What lies under the cloudy skies of Venus? What does Pluto look like? Until we sent a spacecraft there, we didn't know. Since the early days of space exploration, there have been hundreds of important space missions that have discovered new and exciting things. Space exploration has resulted in new inventions and new technologies as scientists and engineers have worked to get rockets, satellites and astronauts into space.

How many times do you turn on the TV or check the weather and take those services for granted? It is hard to imagine life without these inventions, but they both rely on satellites in space.

Another invention, Global Positioning System or GPS, transformed how we navigate and even how countries go to war. When an airplane crashes or a ship gets lost at sea, beacons send the position to space, notifying Search and Rescue. This would not be possible without space missions.

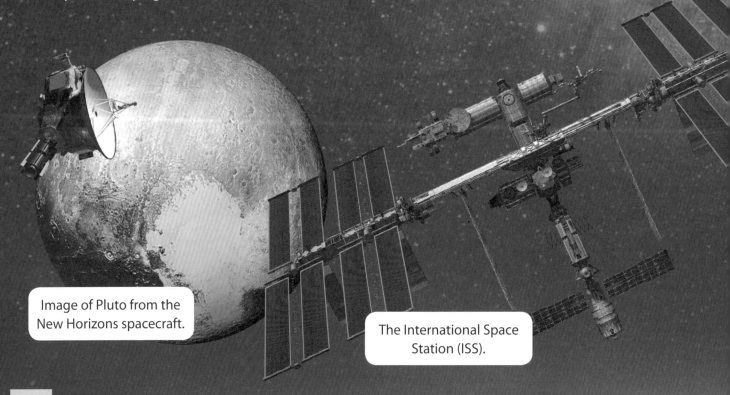

Image of Pluto from the New Horizons spacecraft.

The International Space Station (ISS).

4

The most famous missions were part of the **Space Race** between the former **Soviet Union** and the United States of America. The Space Race was a battle of the superpowers, and both countries wanted to prove they had the best technology. The race to land a human on the Moon was a very big deal, inspiring kids around the world to become scientists and engineers.

This book is an introduction to the vastness of space exploration. By sharing the details of 50 space missions that changed the world, we hope to inspire you to pay attention to future missions. Space history is unfolding right before your eyes!

GPS satellite.

Canadian astronaut Julie Payette gets suited up to launch on the space shuttle for a 10-day mission to the International Space Station.

Rocket Science

Getting into space is really hard! To get to space, and stay there, almost the entire mass of the spacecraft must be fuel. That's why Moon rockets were so huge. They needed to be large to carry all that fuel!

When a spacecraft fires its engines in the vacuum of space there is no air to slow it down. As long as there is fuel, the spacecraft can keep speeding up! After the engines shut off, the spacecraft coasts, following a path determined by gravity. This path is called a **trajectory**. If that trajectory sends the spacecraft around a planet, moon or star, we say the spacecraft is in **orbit**.

Newton's Third Law

Rockets work by shooting hot gases away from the spacecraft. Isaac Newton's Third Law states that "Every action has an equal and opposite reaction." A rocket pushes against the hot gases and the gases push back! This moves the rocket forward.

Spacecraft that go into space but have speeds of less than 28,000 kilometres per hour (km/hr) fall right back to Earth. Rockets that fly to space but fall right back down are called sub-orbital rockets.

Reaction! The rocket moves forward.

Action! A rocket pushes on the gas.

Rocket fuel

Most rockets are powered by liquids like kerosene and liquid oxygen. Some rockets, like the side boosters on the space shuttle, use a solid fuel.

In space travel, gravity is by far the ruling force. Gravity weakens as you go away from a planet or star, but never goes away entirely. In fact, the gravity on astronauts floating in the space station is almost the same as on Earth!

So why do astronauts float? On Earth, we are pulled towards the ground, and in turn, the ground pushes back on us. When a spacecraft is in orbit, it is falling. It just happens to be falling around the Earth. Because astronauts fall along with the spacecraft, the floor of the spacecraft isn't pushing up on the astronauts, and that's why they float!

How high is space?

Space is considered to be anywhere above 100 km. However, if a spacecraft wants to stay in space, it would need to be almost twice that high. Any lower, and there's enough air to slow it down, causing it to fall back to Earth.

Gravity is the attraction felt between objects as they warp the space around them.

It is never correct to say, "there is no gravity in space." For this reason, we use the word **microgravity** for the weightless environment aboard a spacecraft.

Space exploration provides jobs to millions of people all around the world! Government space agencies, like NASA, are only a small part of this huge industry.

There's a lot to learn if you want to work with rockets and spaceships. You may think the most important subjects are physics, chemistry and math. You'd be right, these subjects are important. But so is working as a team as well as good communication skills.

After high school, more training is required before you can get to work. While a degree in engineering, physics or math is required for many space jobs, other skills are also needed. Tradespeople such as welders and metalworkers construct rockets, spacecraft and robots.

Constructing the Boeing CST-100 Starliner spacecraft.

Internships

University physics and engineering programs often offer paid internships where students work on important real-world problems. These internships are often the ticket to the most exciting jobs after graduation.

Engineers prepare to do some welding as they construct a spacecraft at the Michoud Assembly Facility in New Orleans.

CHAPTER 1
Enter the Space Age

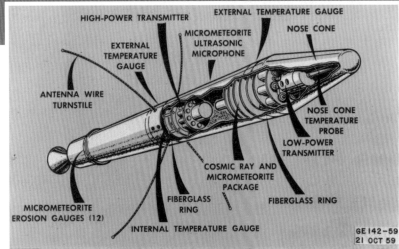

HIGH-POWER TRANSMITTER — EXTERNAL TEMPERATURE GAUGE

MICROMETEORITE ULTRASONIC MICROPHONE

NOSE CONE

EXTERNAL TEMPERATURE GAUGE

ANTENNA WIRE TURNSTILE

NOSE CONE TEMPERATURE PROBE

LOW-POWER TRANSMITTER

COSMIC RAY AND MICROMETEORITE PACKAGE

MICROMETEORITE EROSION GAUGES (12)

FIBERGLASS RING

FIBERGLASS RING

INTERNAL TEMPERATURE GAUGE

GE 142-59
21 OCT 59

EXPLORER I

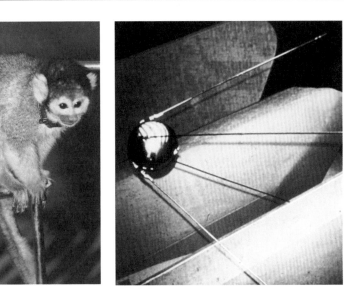

So many rockets! Text: We tend to only hear about the most famous spaceflights, but in the early days of rocketry, there were thousands of small rockets launched to space (But **not** orbit) from many countries as researchers and engineers tried to learn about the new frontier of space. This even included countries like Norway, Sweden, Greece, and Canada!

1 The First Spacecraft

First V-2 flight October 3, 1942

After its defeat in the First World War, Germany wanted to regain its military power by making new and improved weapons. Near the end of the Second World War, Germany created a weapon system called the V-2 rocket. The "V" stands for "Vengeance Weapon." This rocket was the first machine to operate above the Earth's atmosphere. The Space Age had begun!

The V-2 rocket was created by a team headed by an aerospace engineer named Wernher von Braun. It was used to bomb London, England, and Belgium during the Second World War. The V-2 could reach altitudes of over 160 km. It was the first time humans had sent an object into space.

The V-2 was guided by radar beams. Its distance was determined by fuel.

In 1950, captured V-2 rockets were modified for research purposes, and renamed "Bumper" rockets because they carried a second **sounding rocket** on their nose. These were the very first rockets launched from Cape Canaveral in Florida.

The V-2 rocket was powered by potato alcohol, and stabilized by jet vanes, devices positioned within the rocket's exhaust.

Spaceflight in the 1940s

Near the end of the Second World War, many German rocket scientists surrendered and moved to the United States of America. There they designed rockets for the United States Army and, eventually, **NASA**. Other German scientists surrendered to the Soviet Union. Many continued to work on V-2 rockets and on Soviet rocket programs.

First photos from space

This image was taken using a 35-mm video camera mounted atop a captured V-2 rocket.

Wernher von Braun with a model of the V-2 rocket. Although employed by the German army to build rockets, Wernher von Braun was obsessed with spaceflight.

While the Americans were launching captured V-2 rockets, the Soviet Union was launching a nearly identical rocket called the R-1 ballistic missile.

2 Sputnik and the Space Race

October 4, 1957

After the Second World War, a new type of war brewed between the world's superpowers, the United States of America and the Soviet Union. Although the two countries did not engage in direct combat, they were both determined to build the best weapons. This was the **Cold War** and it lasted until 1991.

In war, the army on the highest ground has the advantage, and nothing is higher than space. The United States of America and the Soviet Union raced to control this new frontier, and the Space Race was born.

On October 4, 1957, the Soviet Union became the first nation to send a spacecraft into orbit around the Earth. Its name was Sputnik, and at 58 cm wide, it wasn't much larger than a beach ball. But this was a huge win for the Soviets.

Humans could now send things up to space, and keep them there!

In October 1957, Sputnik became the first spacecraft to orbit the Earth.

Sputnik launched in the very tip of the nose of an R-7 Semyorka rocket.

What was the Soviet Union?

The Soviet Union (USSR) was a group of communist nations joined into a single large country. The largest of these nations was Russia. The USSR broke up in 1991.

Second place in space

With the Soviet Union now able to send a spacecraft into orbit, this meant that at any moment, a nuclear missile could be directed anywhere on Earth. The launch of Sputnik and other large satellites by the Soviets showed that the United States was behind in space exploration! This led the American government to form NASA on July 29, 1958.

America's first satellite was called Explorer 1. It was developed by Jet Propulsion Laboratory (JPL) in California. Explorer 1 launched just four months after Sputnik. Like Sputnik, the spacecraft was tiny, at about 2 metres long and 16 cm wide. Unlike Sputnik, Explorer 1 carried scientific instruments to detect **meteoroids** and **radiation**.

Explorer 1 launched on January 31, 1958.

Canada was the third country to put an artificial satellite into orbit. The spacecraft, named Alouette 1, was launched from California on an American rocket.

Launch of Explorer 1 on a Jupiter rocket.

Alouette 1, Canada's first satellite, launched on September 29, 1962.

3 First Animals in Space

Sputnik II launched on November 3, 1957

One month after Sputnik, Sputnik II launched into orbit around the Earth. A tiny chamber in the nose of the rocket carried Laika, a stray dog from the streets of Moscow. Laika became the first living thing to orbit the Earth.

Many people think that Laika was the first animal in space, but this isn't technically true. Many other animals, including other dogs, travelled to space before Laika without going into orbit.

Although Laika died shortly after entering orbit, the mission proved that it was possible for living creatures to orbit the Earth. This was another win for the Soviet Union in the Cold War with the United States of America.

Albert II was the first primate in space, but his V-2 rocket did not reach orbit.

Animal firsts

The first animals in space were fruit flies launched aboard a V-2 rocket. The first mammal in space was a monkey named Albert II. The first dogs in space were named Tsygan and Deszik.

Laika preparing for flight.

4 First Human in Space

Growing up on a farm outside of Moscow, and living under German occupation during the Second World War, the young Yuri Gagarin could never have imagined that someday he would be the first person to voyage into space.

Yuri was a talented pilot, very smart and well-liked by everyone. He was also very short, at just under 5 feet 2 inches tall. This made him the ideal person to crew the Soviet Vostok spacecraft, which was very small.

The spacecraft Yuri flew to orbit was named Vostok 1. It launched into space on April 12, 1961. During the flight Yuri ate and drank, proving that the human body could work in space. After one orbit around the Earth, **retro rockets** fired, sending the spacecraft back into the atmosphere. As the capsule fell towards Earth, Yuri ejected and parachuted safely to the ground.

Vostok 1, the spaceship that carried Yuri into space.

Yuri Gagarin, first human in space.

MiG-15

Tragedy

The Soviet government tried to keep Yuri safe, banning him from future spaceflights. However, seven years after his record-breaking spaceflight, Yuri died after his MiG-15 fighter jet crashed while on a training flight.

The First Astronaut

Three weeks after Yuri Gagarin's flight, the United States of America launched its first astronaut, Alan Bartlett Shepard Jr., into space on May 5, 1961.

Unlike Gagarin, Shepard didn't go into orbit. The rocket that carried Shepard's Mercury spacecraft was made from a US Army missile. These rockets went to space and fell right back down.

Shepard's spacecraft was named Freedom 7. Despite his flight lasting only 15 minutes, Shepard had a lot to do. During the flight, he changed between manual and automatic control, testing his ability to steer the spacecraft.

Astronaut Alan Shepard awaits lift-off in the Mercury capsule named Freedom 7.

Ten years later, Alan Shepard became the fifth person to walk on the Moon.

The Mercury-Redstone Rocket (MR-3) carrying the Freedom 7 spacecraft.

The previous Mercury flight carried Ham the chimpanzee.

Alan Shepard on the Moon.

16

Friendship 7 launched on February 20, 1962

On February 20, 1962, the United States of America finally placed a human into Earth's orbit. During the flight, John Herschel Glenn Jr. spent almost five hours in space, circling Earth three times. It was a good thing Glenn was a talented pilot, because the spacecraft's automatic control system failed, and he had to fly the spacecraft manually.

When the craft re-entered Earth's atmosphere it began to rock back and forth. The parachute deployed about 2,000 metres too early and the spacecraft strayed from its course. Fortunately, the spacecraft splashed down safely in the Atlantic Ocean and Glenn was rescued by a navy warship. With Glenn safely back on Earth, the United States of America was finally catching up to the Soviet Union.

John Glenn

John Glenn's spacecraft, named Friendship 7, launched atop an Atlas rocket. This same rocket design would later be used to send robotic spacecraft to the Moon, Mars and Venus.

Friendship 7 capsule

Atlas rocket

Mercury 7

Alan Shepard and John Glenn were members of NASA's Mercury 7 — a group of 7 test pilots chosen to be America's first astronauts.

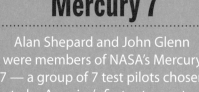

7 The First Spacewalk

Vostok 2 spacewalk, March 18, 1965

Proving that humans could survive in spacesuits outside their spacecraft was an important step in the race to the Moon. However, the first spacewalk by Soviet **cosmonaut** Alexei Leonov almost ended in disaster.

There were two cosmonauts onboard the Vostok 2 spacecraft: Alexei Leonov and Pavel Belyayev. The spacecraft had an airlock that let one person leave the capsule. The mission was simple: conduct the first spacewalk and record it on film.

Alexei Leonov

However, after 10 minutes outside the spacecraft, Leonov's spacesuit began to swell. It became difficult to bend his arms and legs and he was unable to fit his body back into the airlock!

Letting some air out of the suit, he entered the airlock headfirst but had trouble turning around to close the hatch. After a struggle, he was finally able to close the airlock hatch and re-enter the spacecraft.

Alexei Leonov outside the Vostok 2 on the first spacewalk.

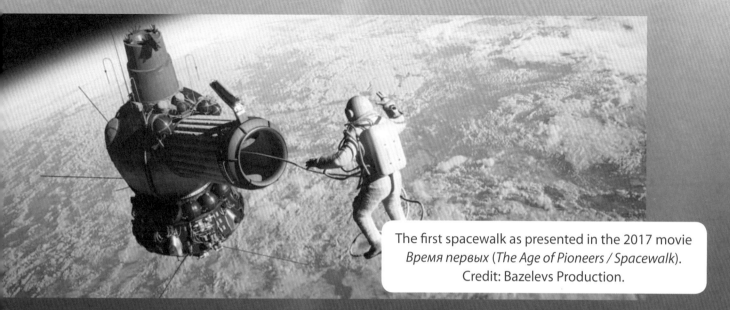

The first spacewalk as presented in the 2017 movie *Время первых* (*The Age of Pioneers / Spacewalk*). Credit: Bazelevs Production.

An unexpected adventure

The troubles didn't end there. During re-entry into Earth's atmosphere, the spacecraft's guidance system failed, and the crew landed in a remote forest, thousands of kilometres from where they were supposed to be.

For the next two days, they fought a broken hatch, a snowstorm, freezing temperatures and the threat of wild animals. Eventually, the cosmonauts' location was discovered by aircraft and supplies were dropped from the sky. The next morning, a recovery team arrived on skis, leading the cosmonauts to a waiting helicopter.

Despite the difficulties, this mission proved that spacewalks were possible.

"Provided with a special suit, man can survive and work in open space. Thank you for your attention." — Alexei Leonov.

American astronaut Ed White performed America's first spacewalk on June 3, 1965.

8 The First Spy Satellite

Discovery 13 launched on August 10, 1960

When the United States of America's **atom bomb** effectively ended the Second World War, it proved that advanced weapons win wars. By 1949, the Soviet Union had atom bombs, too.

The United States of America wanted information about Soviet weapons. They had spy planes, but those could be shot down. They knew the future of spying would be from space. The first spy satellite was named Corona. Its first successful mission, called Discovery 13, launched on August 10, 1960, and it forever changed how the United States of America spies on its enemies.

There were no digital cameras in 1960, so the spy satellites used film. To get the film back to Earth, the film canisters were ejected from the spacecraft. While descending by parachute, the canisters would be snagged from the air by a plane. The film canisters had a built-in self-destruct system in case they were lost.

Corona, the first spy satellite.

C-119 aircraft training to recover a film canister.

Secret Space Stations

first space station was named Salyut 1 and launched in April 1971. It was built by the Soviet Union ng the Cold War. The Soviets claimed that these early space stations were peaceful science mission ever, we later learned the Salyut 3 station was armed with a 23-mm cannon! The Soviet Union bui these space stations, 7 of them were operational, but all paved the way for the much larger statior ome.

Salyut 1 spent 175 days in orbit. Cosmonauts flew to the station on separate spacecraft. The first group of cosmonauts to reach the station were unable to dock and had to return to Earth. The second group of cosmonauts docked successfully. Their job was to test the space station's systems. However, on their way back to Earth, their mission ended in tragedy. The spacecraft lost air pressure, exposing them to th vacuum of space. The spacecraft parachuted to Eart as planned, but the crew had perished.

A Soyuz pacecraft delivering ew to the ce station.

Salyut 7, an early Soviet space station.

Saving Salyut 7

Salyut 7 was the last of the secret Soviet space stations. In 1985, while the station was between crews, it suffered a malfunction and began to spin. Worried that the station might fall into American hands, the Soviet Union sent a crew on a daring mission and revived the station! After the repair, this space station operated for another six years.

Death in space

Georgy Dobrovolsky, Vladislav Volkov and Viktor Patsayev, the crew of Soyuz 11, are the only people to have died in space.

A Progress resupply spacecraft docked at the second port.

10 First Woman in Space

June 16, 1963

On June 16, 1963, a 26-year-old woman named Valentina Tereshkova launched into space atop a Soviet Vostok rocket. She was chosen to be a cosmonaut because of her experience as a skydiver. Early Soviet spacecraft required the cosmonaut to eject from the spacecraft during descent and parachute back to Earth.

Her flight lasted almost three days, during which she circled the Earth 48 times. The flight was used to study the effects of space travel on the female body, proving that women could be cosmonauts, too. Upon re-entering Earth's atmosphere, she ejected from the spacecraft and parachuted to the ground.

It was 19 years before the next woman, cosmonaut Svetlana Savitskaya, flew into space on a mission to the Salyut 7 space station.

Cosmonaut

The word cosmonaut is formed by the combination of two Greek words: "cosmos" meaning space and "nautes" meaning sailor.

"A bird cannot fly with one wing only. Human spaceflight cannot develop any further without the active participation of women." — Valentina Tereshkova

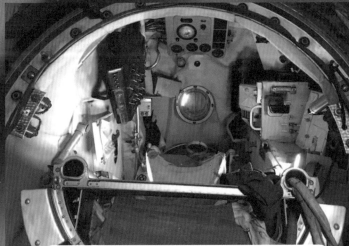

Inside the Vostok 6 capsule. Tereshkova's spacecraft's call-sign was Chaika, which means "Seagull."

CHAPTER 2
Race to the Moon

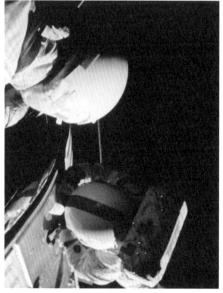

Moon rockets were fast!

Escape **velocity** is the speed a spacecraft must reach (at the moment it shuts off its engines) to coast away from a planet. For an object starting from Earth, this speed is about 40,000 km/hr.

11 Humans Orbit the Moon

Of all the voyages in human history, Apollo 8 might have been the boldest, the most dangerous and had the most at stake. The Soviets had just launched a new spacecraft to the Moon and they were about to put two humans on the next flight. The United States of America wanted to get there first.

On December 21, 1968, three US astronauts, Frank Borman, James A. Lovell and William Anders, launched into space. It was the first crewed mission of the new Saturn V rocket, and the first time humans had ever left **low Earth orbit**. It was also the first time humans had orbited the Moon.

Saturn V rocket launching Apollo 8.

Bill Anders inside the Apollo 8 command module.

James Lovell at the command module's navigation station.

An "Out of this World" Christmas

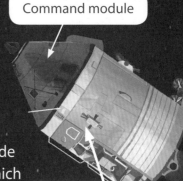

Command module

Service module

Borman, Lovell and Anders arrived in lunar orbit on Christmas Eve, delivering a televised address to the world. They circled the Moon 20 times, taking photographs and doing other work in preparation for the landing mission planned for the very next year.

The trip wasn't free of trouble. Borman was sick with vomiting and diarrhea. All three astronauts had trouble sleeping. Debris from spent rocket stages made navigation a challenge. A computer issue caused a **thruster** to fire in error, which could have forced the spacecraft into a deadly spin.

At the end of their six-day journey, the spacecraft splashed down into choppy seas. It floated upside down for nearly ten minutes before righting itself. When the rescue crew arrived, they opened the hatch, but were driven back by the horrible smell they found inside!

Why go to the Moon?

"Kennedy had taken the view that if the United States of America were to lead what he called the free world, it must prove that it was more capable than its rival."
— Brian Harvey, author of
Soviet and Russian Lunar Exploration

Earth rise. The astronauts of Apollo 8 were the first humans in history to witness an Earth rise. Anders took this photo, which became one of the most famous images of all time.

12 Humans on the Moon

Six hundred million people around the world watched Neil Armstrong step out of Apollo 11's lunar module and set foot upon the Moon. The preparations for that small step took hundreds of thousands of people from all over the world.

The Apollo 11 mission was launched from the Kennedy Space Center on July 16, 1969. People gathered along roadways and in fields and on beaches along the Florida coast as Neil Armstrong, Edwin "Buzz" Aldrin and Michael Collins lifted off aboard the Saturn V rocket.

One of the first footprints on the Moon.

It took only 12 minutes to get the spacecraft into Earth's orbit. The crew circled the Earth until their spacecraft was pointed just right so that the rocket's third stage could blast them towards the Moon at over 37,000 km/hr.

Building a lunar module.

Three days later, the command module's engine fired, placing the spacecraft in orbit around the Moon.

Armstrong and Aldrin entered the lunar lander, leaving Collins behind to fly the command module. An engine on the lunar module slowed the lander down so that it would descend to the Moon's surface.

The Apollo 11 command and service modules shortly after construction.

26

"The *Eagle* has landed"

Landing occurred at 4:17 p.m. Eastern Standard Time, July 20, 1969.

Armstrong and Aldrin spent just under 22 hours on the Moon, spending two and a half hours walking on the lunar surface. During their time on the surface, they planted the American flag, took pictures and collected rock samples. They also set up experiments to detect Moon quakes and a device used to calculate the exact distance to the Moon.

With the bottom half of the lunar lander serving as a launch pad, Armstrong and Aldrin blasted off the surface. Four hours later, they docked with the command module, rejoining Collins.

Buzz Aldrin climbs down the lander towards the lunar surface.

Apollo 11's lunar lander was named *Eagle*. However, as soon as it touched down on the Moon, it became Tranquility Base.

Aldrin (left) and Armstrong (right) in the lunar module

The command module was named *Columbia*.

Launch abort system

Service module

From 1968 to 1972, there were nine crewed missions to the Moon. Six of these missions landed humans on the surface. There were so many important firsts during these flights that dozens, if not hundreds of books have been written about these missions. Thousands of scientific papers were written from the experiments the astronauts set up, and more are still being written to this day.

The "dress rehearsal" — Apollo 10

This mission was the first to fly the lunar lander to the Moon, but the astronauts were not given enough fuel to land. The lunar module was nicknamed Snoopy.

Launched May 18, 1969

The pranksters — Apollo 12

The Apollo 12 crew had a reputation for being the funniest. Lots of practical jokes were played onboard this mission. Astronaut Pete Conrad was particularly known for his pranks. One such prank included a plastic toy cockroach hidden in the spacecraft.

Launched November 14, 1969

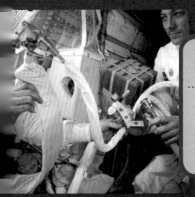

The "life boat" — Apollo 13

This mission experienced an explosion in one of the oxygen tanks and was not able to land on the Moon. The supplies on the lunar module were used to get the astronauts home. The astronauts had to make a custom filter to clean the air of carbon dioxide so they could continue to breathe.

Launched April 11, 1970

The "golfer" — Apollo 14

Astronaut Alan Shepard (first American in space) brought the head of a six-iron golf club and two golf balls. He built a club out of a shovel and, while out on the lunar surface, hit the balls as far as he could (check out the video on YouTube!).

Launched January 31, 1971

"Cars on the Moon" — Apollo 15

Apollo 15 brought the first of three "Moon Buggies" to the lunar surface. These battery-powered cars carried the astronauts several kilometres from their base. The cars had a video camera that could be controlled from Mission Control on Earth.

Launched July 26, 1971

Mattingly collects film canisters during a spacewalk.

Moon walks and a spacewalk — Apollo 16

Apollo 16 was a busy mission. With almost three days on the lunar surface, driving almost 27 km in the lunar rover, the whole mission lasted over 11 days! Not only did the astronauts conduct three **extra-vehicular activities (EVA)**, but once in orbit, astronaut Ken Mattingly performed a spacewalk to retrieve film canisters from cameras located around the spacecraft.

Launched April 16, 1972

Lone scientist — Apollo 17

A geologist named Harrison Schmitt was on Apollo 17, the last Apollo mission to the Moon. Of the 12 people that have walked on the surface of the Moon (as of this writing), Schmitt was the only scientist.

Launched December 7, 1972

14 "Moon Walker" Robots

Lunokhod 1 launched on November 10, 1970

While the Americans were launching crewed missions to the Moon, the Soviet Union launched the first robotic Moon rover to prepare for future crewed Soviet missions (that were later cancelled).

The rover, named Lunokhod (which means "lunar traveller"), was huge — over four metres long and two metres high. The rover had nine wheels. One was used to measure distance, the other eight were each driven by an electric motor. If one of the wheels were to jam, an explosive charge would blow it clear of the rover.

Moon tortoises

Instead of people, the Soviets' first crew-capable Moon spaceship carried two tortoises. Russia has still not sent humans to the Moon.

The rover was equipped with cameras and television cameras, and a variety of scientific instruments. It was driven by a team of five people back on Earth. A second rover, Lunokhod 2, landed on the Moon in January 1973. It lasted four months on the lunar surface in the Sea of Serenity, driving a total distance of 37 km.

People living in the Soviet Union didn't get much news about the American missions, so for Soviet children it was the news of these rovers that inspired the next generation of explorers.

Teamwork In Space

Apollo-Soyuz launched on July 15, 1975

After the United States of America had completed the Apollo Moon missions, NASA had an extra spacecraft, left over from the cancelled Apollo 18 mission. They used this spacecraft to complete the first international, crewed space mission — the Apollo-Soyuz Test Project. This joint mission by the United States of America and Soviet Union paved the way for a future of teamwork in space.

On July 15, 1975, the two spacecraft launched from opposite sides of the planet. From Florida, an Apollo command module launched with three astronauts, Thomas Stafford, Vance Brand and Donald "Deke" Slayton. In Kazakhstan, a Soyuz spacecraft lifted off with two cosmonauts, Alexei Leonov (who conducted the first spacewalk) and Valeri Kubasov.

It took two days for the spacecraft to meet. A special docking port was designed to connect the two spacecraft. They remained docked together for almost two days. During the joint mission, the astronauts and cosmonauts exchanged gifts, toured each other's spacecraft and did experiments.

Learning Russian

When visiting the International Space Station today, astronauts and cosmonauts are expected to converse in both English and Russian.

CHAPTER 3
Exploring the Solar System

Illustration of the Cassini spacecraft as it arrives at Saturn.

16 First to Mercury

The first mission to Mercury launched on November 3, 1973. The spacecraft didn't have enough fuel to stop and orbit the planet. Instead, the Mariner 10 spacecraft circled the Sun, passing by Mercury on each lap.

For the first time, humans glimpsed the details of the planet's surface. At first, Mercury looked much like our Moon, but look more closely and much of Mercury's landscape looks like melting ice. But why? This is because it's so hot on Mercury that the rocks are slowly turning to gas, and this process makes them look shiny!

The large craters on Mercury's surface were soon named after famous artists. Three of the largest craters are named for Beethoven the musician, Homer the Greek poet and Victor Hugo, the author.

NASA's Mariner 10 spacecraft.

First close-up image of Mercury taken by the Mariner 10 spacecraft.

17 Under Venus's Clouds

The first spacecraft to reach Venus, and enter its atmosphere, was a Soviet Union spacecraft named Venera 4. A later spacecraft, Venera 7, reached the surface. It wasn't until Venera 9 that a photograph of Venus's surface was taken.

Now we know that Venus is not a great place to live. It rains sulfuric acid, the atmosphere is very thick and the temperature is hot enough to melt lead! Even the probes that reached the surface lasted, at most, little more than an hour.

A view from the surface. This image, showing a very rocky landscape, is from the Venera 9 spacecraft.

Mapped with radar

Because of the thick clouds, it is impossible to take images of Venus's surface from space with regular light. A spacecraft named Magellan used radar to get detailed, three dimensional (3D) maps of the surface of the planet.

This illustration shows a Venera lander on the surface of Venus (illustrated by Reimund Bertrams).

18 First to Mars

Before Mars was visited by spacecraft, many people believed it was inhabited by Martians! Early Martian maps showed canals, and people thought these were a giant alien engineering project. Then, in 1965, the Mariner 4 spacecraft took the first up-close images of Mars and we learned that Mars was a desert, devoid of life.

The Mariner 4 spacecraft was able to measure the atmosphere, which is one hundred times thinner than Earth's. It also measured daytime surface temperatures of less than -100° Celsius! No evidence of aliens was discovered on the surface.

Mariner 4 spacecraft

Not so digital photography

When the data came back from the first images (which it did very slowly), scientists were so eager to see the Martian surface that they filled in a grid, by hand, using colour pastel!

19 On the Martian Surface

The Soviet Union landed a spacecraft, and a rover, on Mars in 1971, but its signal was lost seconds after landing. The first successful Mars landing was a NASA spacecraft named Viking 1, which reached Mars in 1976. It sent data back to Earth for the next six years!

The Viking orbiter stayed in space while a lander touched down on the planet's surface. The lander had a robotic arm for collecting soil samples, a weather station, a **seismometer** to listen for Marsquakes and other scientific instruments.

Viking orbiter

Viking 1 discovered that the soil on Mars was volcanic in nature. It also discovered evidence of an ancient riverbed. Later missions found proof that Mars once had oceans with liquid water in them.

This image was taken during a Martian sunset by the Viking 1 lander.

Viking 1 launched on August 20, 1975.

Face on Mars?

Can you see the face in this Viking 1 image? It is caused by shadows on a mountain. It is an example of pareidolia — a tendency for humans to see patterns in objects.

20 First to Jupiter

Pioneer 10 was the first spacecraft to travel beyond Mars and give the world its first close-up view of the "Gas Giant," Jupiter.

The spacecraft launched in 1972, rocketing away from Earth with so much velocity that it passed the Moon's orbit in only 11 hours. It reached its highest speeds while zipping past Jupiter at over 132,000 km/hr!

During the spacecraft's encounter with Jupiter, Pioneer 10 took the first close-up images of the planet and its four largest moons. The spacecraft also carried instruments to measure the planet's **magnetic field** and radiation.

After its fly-by with Jupiter, Pioneer 10 was sent on a path that would take it out of the Solar System! The spacecraft continued to transmit data until 2003, 30 years after its launch.

Illustration of the Pioneer 10 spacecraft

Pioneer took this image of Jupiter at a distance of 2.5 million km.

Pioneer 10 prepares for launch aboard an Atlas-Centaura rocket.

One hot planet

Pioneer 10 discovered that Jupiter emits more heat than it receives from the Sun!

21 The Grand Tour

If there is one space mission as epic as the Moon landing, this is it. The two Voyager spacecraft have visited four planets and dozens of moons — and continue to do science today, 45 years after their launch! Voyager 1 launched on September 5, 1977, while Voyager 2 launched weeks earlier on August 20.

Uranus's moon Miranda.

Voyager 1 visited Jupiter and Saturn and Voyager 2 visited Jupiter, Saturn, Uranus and Neptune. Voyager 2 is the only spacecraft to have visited the "Ice Giants," Uranus and Neptune.

The mission discovered active volcanoes on Jupiter's moon Io, studied Saturn's rings and analyzed Titan's atmosphere. Titan is Saturn's largest moon. Voyager 2 got a close look at Uranus's moon Miranda. It discovered 1,000-km/hr winds on Neptune and a great storm in the southern portion of the planet. It also found active **geysers** on Neptune's icy moon, Triton.

After their mission to the planets, the spacecraft continued on their path through our Solar System and beyond. As of 2020, both spacecraft are still transmitting data back to Earth.

A Voyager spacecraft.

Close-up view of Neptune's moon Triton.

Saturn

Uranus

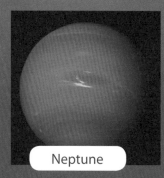
Neptune

Io, a moon covered in volcanoes

A blue dot and a golden record

The white arrow above points at Earth in an image taken by Voyager 1 on July 6, 1990, from 6 billion km away! It has become one of the most famous photographs ever. The image inspired a scientist named Carl Sagan to say, "Look again at that dot. That's here. That's home . . . To me, it underscores our responsibility to deal more kindly with one another, and to preserve and cherish the pale blue dot, the only home we've ever known."

The golden records

Each of the Voyager spacecraft carries with them a golden record, to tell a human story to any aliens who might find the spacecraft. The record also serves as a message of hope for those of us on Earth. The records contain music by Mozart, nature sounds like thunder and human sounds like greetings and laughter.

22 Driving on Mars

These roving robots have inspired LEGO kits, cartoon characters and science enthusiasts the world over. Who is driving these rovers? A team of engineers at NASA's Jet Propulsion Laboratory in California!

The first successful Mars rover was named Sojourner. It landed on Mars in 1997, spending 83 Martian days exploring the surface. Sojourner was small, only 11.5 kilograms. During its 100-metre drive, it took 550 pictures and conducted 15 detailed rock analyses.

The Mars Exploration Rover Mission is probably the most overachieving mission in NASA's history. Two solar-powered rovers, named Spirit and Opportunity, were intended to explore the Martian surface for 90 days. Both spacecraft launched in 2003 and landed on Mars in 2004. Spirit was operational until 2010, and Opportunity was operated until 2018!

Sojourner rover launched on December 4, 1996.

Opportunity rover launched on July 8, 2003.

Airbags!

The Sojourner, Spirit and Opportunity rovers didn't so much land on Mars as bounce. The rovers were wrapped in inflatable lobes, like giant balloons. When the bouncing stopped, the airbags deflated and the rover emerged, ready to explore!

Bigger and better

The Curiosity rover is almost three metres long and over two metres tall. That's about as long, and nearly twice as tall, as the lunar roving vehicle used by the astronauts during the Apollo missions to the Moon! Curiosity is powered by plutonium (a radioactive metal) and has radios powerful enough to reach the Earth without a relay satellite.

This rover, which landed in 2012, has 17 cameras and can even take high definition (HD) video. Its two-metre-long robotic arm contains five different tools, including rock drills and dirt scoops. The Curiosity rover was too large to land using the airbag method. Instead a "Sky-Crane" lowered it to the surface.

Sky-Crane lowers the Curiosity rover to the surface.

Curiosity rover launched on November 26, 2011.

Curiosity rover can shoot a laser from its mast to analyze rock samples.

23 Up Close to Saturn

Cassini launched on October 15, 1997

Magnificent Saturn is beautiful through any small telescope. But now we have much more detailed information about the planet and its 53 moons. The Cassini spacecraft launched in 1997 and took almost 7 years to reach Saturn. It then spent 13 years exploring the planet, its rings and its moons.

Cassini's amazing journey to Saturn began with a trip to Venus and back past Earth again, using energy from these planets to pick up speed. Then it went past the Moon, close to an asteroid and past Jupiter.

The spacecraft visited many of Saturn's moons, and even flew between the gaps in Saturn's rings. Using radar, it created a detailed map of Saturn's largest moon, Titan, discovering lakes of liquid methane (a **hydrocarbon**).

The Cassini Mission was controlled from the Space Flight Operation Center at NASA's Jet Propulsion Laboratory in Pasadena, California.

Cassini spacecraft

Landing on Titan

The Cassini spacecraft carried a very special passenger, a probe named Huygens. This probe was dropped from the mother ship, and sailed into Titan's atmosphere, parachuting down to the surface of Saturn's moon.

On the way down, the 1.3-metre-wide probe took images of the surface, showing what looked like rivers flowing into a lake. There is no liquid water on Titan (it is -200°C). Instead the rivers and lakes are filled with liquid hydrocarbons. The probe landed on the lake shore, taking temperature readings and images of pebbles made of ice.

Illustration of Huygens probe on Titan's surface.

Image of Titan's rivers and lakes.

Smile!

As a tribute to Voyager 1's Pale Blue Dot photo, Cassini took this photo of Earth beneath Saturn's rings. The image was conceived by Carolyn Porco at the Space Science Institute and dedicated to the late Carl Sagan.

24 Visiting Halley's Comet

Comets are city-sized balls of ice and dust that form long tails as the Sun heats up their surface. The most famous comet is Halley's Comet, which appears in our night sky every 76 years. It was named after Edwin Halley, the astronomer who predicted its return — one of the most famous predictions in scientific history!

In 1986, a European spacecraft named Giotto visited Halley's Comet. The Giotto probe discovered that the comet was 80 per cent water! But when the spacecraft came within sight of the comet's nucleus, researchers were shocked by what they saw. The comet was black! For this reason, comets are nicknamed "dirty snowballs."

As Giotto got even closer to the comet, it was hit by a piece of debris. The spacecraft started to spin out of control and engineers thought the mission might be over! Thankfully Giotto's thrusters stabilized the spacecraft and it was soon back to work, taking pictures and doing science.

Giotto probe

Close-up image of Halley's Comet taken by the Giotto spacecraft.

Japan, Russia and France also sent spacecraft to meet the comet.

Japan's Sakigake probe was the first deep space probe to be launched by a country other than the United States or the Soviet Union.

Halley's Comet imaged with a glass plate in 1910 from Peru.

25 Ion Drive

September 27, 2007

Vesta and Ceres are two minor planets located between the orbits of Mars and Jupiter. Discovered only about 200 years ago, these worlds are visible in any backyard telescope. They look like dim stars that change position each night.

In 2007, NASA launched a probe named Dawn. Not only did this spacecraft visit and orbit the two unexplored worlds, it used a special spaceship engine, one that would change the way we travel through space. The engine is an ion drive that pushes gases using electricity instead of burning fuel. In the future, these electric engines may be used to send humans to Mars or to other planets. The ion drive was first used in 1998 on a demonstration mission called Deep Space 1.

Vesta

Ion drives are hundreds of times more efficient than traditional rockets.

Ceres

Dawn probe

26 #CometLanding

It took 10 years for a European spacecraft named Rosetta to reach comet named 67P. The spacecraft stayed with 67P for two years, staying with the comet as it swooped around the Sun and back towards Jupiter.

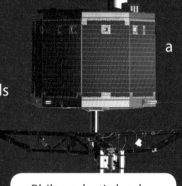

a

Rosetta carried a robotic lander named Philae. In November 2014, Philae floated down to the surface of the comet. News spread quickly around the world and millions of people followed the landing live on social media.

Philae robotic lander.

Philae had three harpoons that were supposed to grab onto the comet, holding the lander in place. Sadly, the harpoons failed to fire, and the spacecraft bounced off the surface, and back into space. Eventually, Philae floated back down to the comet, coming to rest in a crevasse.

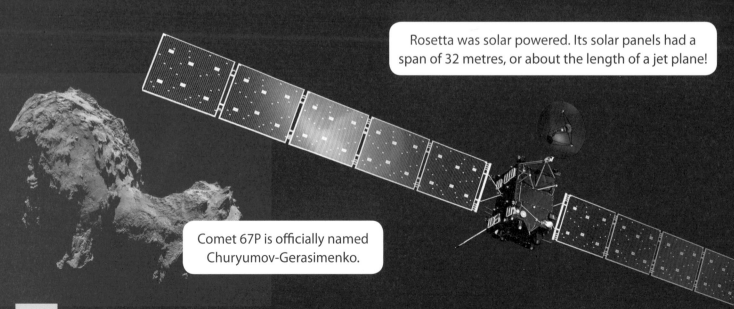

Rosetta was solar powered. Its solar panels had a span of 32 metres, or about the length of a jet plane!

Comet 67P is officially named Churyumov-Gerasimenko.

46

Since its discovery in 1930, Pluto has captured the world's imagination, even inspiring Disney to name a dog after it. However, Pluto is so small, and so far away, that it appears as no more than a dot in even the largest telescopes.

In 2006, a tiny spacecraft named New Horizons launched to explore Pluto for the first time. The spacecraft left Earth travelling at almost 60,000 km/hr, passing the Moon in just nine hours. On its way to Pluto, New Horizons passed by Jupiter, boosting its speed to 83,000 km/hr.

At these incredible speeds, New Horizons reached Pluto in 9 years, after traveling over 5 billion km!

New Horizons

Pluto is so distant that sending a command to the spacecraft, and receiving a response, takes 10 hours using radio signals that travel at the speed of light!

When the first close-up image of Pluto arrived, the scientists were shocked by what they saw. On its side was a giant heart!

Is Pluto a planet?

In 2006, astronomers invented a new way to classify planets. Under these new rules, Pluto was reclassified as a dwarf planet.

28 Touching the Sun!

August 12, 2018

What if you could reach out and touch a star? Many dream of visiting Mars, but there's a very special group of scientists who want to touch the Sun! With the 2018 launch of NASA's Parker Solar Probe, they're about to see their dreams come true.

The Parker Probe is like a weather satellite for our Sun. The Sun can expel particles at over 8 million km/hr. When these particles reach Earth, they can affect our power grids and communications systems. Researchers want to learn more about the outer layers of the Sun (the corona) and solar winds.

Getting close to the Sun takes a lot of speed and energy. On every lap around the Sun, the Parker Probe passes by Venus, getting a boost of speed. The spacecraft is the closest any human-made object has been to the Sun.

Launch of the Parker Solar Probe on a Delta IV heavy rocket.

An 11-cm-thick shield protects the spacecraft from the Sun's heat.

CHAPTER 4
Spacecraft at Work

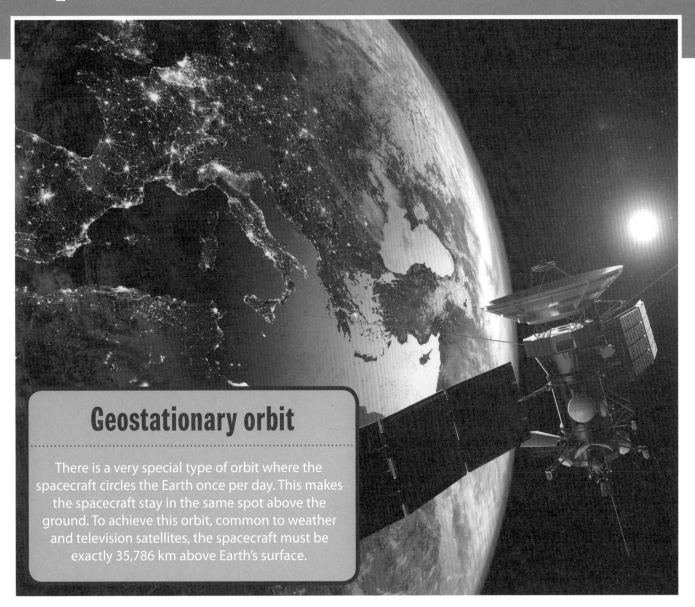

Geostationary orbit

There is a very special type of orbit where the spacecraft circles the Earth once per day. This makes the spacecraft stay in the same spot above the ground. To achieve this orbit, common to weather and television satellites, the spacecraft must be exactly 35,786 km above Earth's surface.

Space Laboratory

Skylab launched on May 14, 1973

The first American space station, named Skylab, was launched in 1973 on a leftover Saturn V rocket from the Moon missions. Even the body of the space station was recycled. It was built from the third stage of the Saturn V Moon rocket.

Compared to the secret Soviet Union space stations, Skylab was much larger and more comfortable. There were spaces onboard that were so roomy, an astronaut could get stuck in midair with the walls completely out of reach! Skylab proved that humans could live and work for long periods of time in space.

To keep their muscles and bones strong, astronauts need to exercise in space so the station had exercise equipment onboard. Skylab even had a toilet and a shower. (On earlier missions, going to the bathroom in space involved tubes, diapers and Ziploc bags!)

Astronaut Charles Conrad Jr. in Skylab's shower.

Shower in space

Skylab even had a shower! However, a shower on a spaceship is not a very good use of water, a precious resource in space. It's also a danger to the spacecraft's electronics. For this reason, the International Space Station does not have a shower.

First American space station

The Skylab space station was a laboratory, with hundreds of different experiments being performed during the station's lifetime. Many of these experiments studied how the human body reacts to long-term weightlessness, but there were also 19 student experiments, including one with spiders building webs in space.

See for yourself

A second Skylab space station was built, but never flown due to a lack of funding. You can visit and even go inside this space station at the National Air and Space Museum in Washington, D.C.

To get to Skylab, astronauts launched aboard a Saturn 1B rocket.

Launch of Skylab on the Saturn V rocket.

The big X

The "X" on Skylab was a separate spacecraft called the Apollo Telescope Mount or ATM. The ATM was a telescope designed to study the Sun. The ATM's cameras used film, which had to be retrieved by spacewalking astronauts.

30 Satellite Television

July 10, 1962

In the early days of television, there were no more than a few television stations. Television was local, broadcast using radio towers and received by an antenna at the viewer's home or through a cable. Satellites changed that forever, enabling live television broadcasts from all over the world and giving viewers access to hundred of channels.

The first television satellite was launched in 1962 and was named Telstar. Telstar's only purpose was to relay a single television signal. Unlike modern television satellites located at fixed points high above Earth, Telstar 1 orbited about every 3 hours.

Within a few weeks of the launch, Telstar was used to relay the first live television signal across the Atlantic. The first broadcast included messages from several American and British news anchors, footage from a baseball game and concluded with a message from US President John F. Kennedy.

Telstar

The Thor-Delta rocket used to launch Telstar 1. The Thor missile acts as the first stage, while Delta is the second stage, which carries the satellite to its final orbit.

Telstar 1's demise

Around the time of the launch of Telstar 1, the United States military detonated a nuclear weapon named "Starfish Prime" in space. The explosion's aftermath damaged three satellites, including Telstar 1.

The nuclear missile that destroyed Telstar 1 rode atop a Thor rocket.

31 Weather Satellites

TIROS launched on April 1, 1960

One of the first uses of images from space was to predict the weather. People knew that if they could track an approaching hurricane with several days notice, people could prepare and thousands of lives could be saved.

Two years after the United States launched its very first satellite, the first weather satellite, TIROS-1, was launched into orbit in 1960. It was the first of several weather satellites bearing the TIROS name (TIROS stands for Television Infrared Observation Satellite).

TIROS satellite

The TIROS-1 used tape recorders to store data from two television cameras. It orbited Earth at about 7,000 km in altitude. The TIROS-1 mission lasted 78 days, proving that weather information could be gathered from space. The 122-kilogram spacecraft still orbits Earth today and is now considered space junk!

TIROS satellites used magnetic tape to record video, but sent still images back to Earth when they passed over a receiving station.

The first weather satellite image was of Atlantic Canada.

32 GPS Navigation

Navstar 1 launched on February 22, 1978

Today, we take the Global Positioning System for granted. GPS technology is in our phones, it's in our watches, it's even in our toys! It is how planes and ships navigate. It is used in construction, farming and tracking endangered species.

GPS became operational in the mid-1990s, but the first GPS satellite, named Navstar 1, was launched on February 22, 1978. Today, there are almost three dozen operational GPS satellites.

GPS was invented by the United States Air Force's Space Command. The most advanced weapon of the Second World War, the V-2 missile, was lucky to get within 5 km of its target. With GPS, a bomb or missile can hit a target within a few centimetres! GPS is under American control and can be turned off over enemy territory. As a result, other nations have developed their own global navigation systems.

GPS satellite

How does GPS work?

GPS satellites broadcast their position and the time. GPS devices, like a cell phone, use this information to determine the distance to each satellite. By knowing the distance to four satellites, your phone can then calculate your position, and display your location on the screen.

Not long ago, sailors could set out to sea and never be heard from again. Hikers sometimes went missing and were never found, and planes would crash without a trace.

In 1979, the Soviet Union, the United States of America, Canada and France got together to end this problem forever. They created a global satellite-based search and rescue system named Cospas-Sarsat. Today, boats and airplanes carry beacons. In an emergency, the beacon transmits a distress signal. A spacecraft sends a message to mission controllers, who dispatch a rescue team.

The first search and rescue spacecraft launched on June 29, 1982. Within a few months, the system was already saving lives. It now includes almost 50 satellites and is integrated with GPS. Forty years since its inception, the Cospas-Sarsat system is credited with saving tens of thousands of lives.

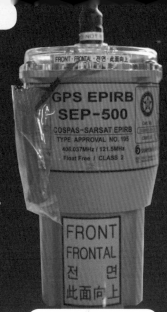

406 MHz distress beacon.

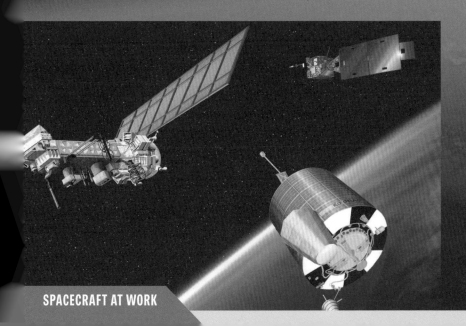

This Cormorant helicopter is used for search and rescue operations in Canada.

34 The Earth from Space

Satellites have been photographing Earth for over 60 years. One of the first Earth-imaging missions was called Landsat. Launched on July 23, 1972, Landsat could view the surface of the Earth with a resolution of 80 metres. It was designed to show how land changes with time due to natural and human activity.

Landsat is a joint venture between NASA and the United States Geological Survey. The imagery has thousands of uses. Farmers can check to see how their crops are doing. Researchers monitor droughts and deforestation. Urban planners use images to design cities. With over 50 years of images, climate-change researchers can track the melting of glaciers and Arctic sea ice.

Landsat images can be viewed through the EarthExplorer website.

Landsat 8 launched on February 11, 2013.

Remote sensing

Using satellites to analyze Earth's systems from space is called remote sensing. For example, this map shows the reduction in Arctic ice between 1979 and 2019.

Modern imaging satellites like Worldview-3 can capture details on Earth as small as 31 centimetres.

35 Exploring the Oceans

There's so much we don't know about our oceans. But it is impossible for submarines and ships to explore all 360 million square km of water. That's why some of the most important ocean research is conducted from space!

Researchers have been using spacecraft to monitor the health of the world's oceans since the late 1970s. The first ocean research spacecraft was named SeaSat. It stayed in space for about 15 weeks.

In recent years, the United States of America and France have partnered on a series of ocean research spacecraft called Jason. This stands for Joint Altimetry Satellite Oceanography Network.

Jason-3 ocean research spacecraft launched on January 17, 2016.

Mapping chlorophyll from space tells researchers where ocean life is thriving or dying.

SeaSat

36 Tiny Satellites

June 30, 2003

Typical satellites cost around $100 million to launch and are owned by big companies. So how can smaller organizations, like universities, ever afford this on their own? The answer is to make the spacecraft small and to send many into space at the same time. These small and relatively cheap satellites are called CubeSats, and they have opened the door for almost anyone to send a spacecraft into space.

The cube-shaped spacecraft are only 10 centimetres to a side! Most of the time, these satellites **piggyback** aboard a rocket carrying a larger satellite. The rocket spits them out before the larger spacecraft is delivered to its final orbit. CubeSats can also be ejected from the space station.

The first cube satellite was launched in 2003 aboard a Russian Rokot rocket. Since that time, over 1,000 of these tiny spaceships have been sent to space to conduct various types of experiments.

CubeSats don't have engines. Over a period of about a year, the spacecraft slow down due to atmospheric drag and fall back to Earth.

37 Riding a Sunbeam

Just as waves at sea can push along a boat, light waves can be used to push a spacecraft. When light hits an object, the light's energy actually gives the object a slight push! The force is very soft, several thousand times weaker than a piece of paper resting on your hand. But construct a large enough sail, and it can move a spaceship!

This tiny force, applied over several months, can speed up a craft by thousands of km/hr! In the future, explorers may use lasers on the Moon or asteroids to push the sail even faster. One day, this technology may allow humans to sail between the stars.

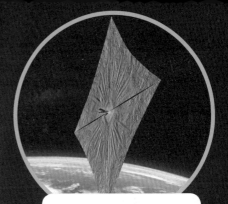

This solar sail, called LightSail 2, was deployed from a cube satellite in 2019.

The first successful solar sail was a Japanese spacecraft called IKAROS, which stands for Interplanetary Kite-craft Accelerated by Radiation of the Sun. Once in space, the spacecraft released a 196-square-metre sail. The sail was part of a demonstration to prove a solar sail could be used for interplanetary flight. IKAROS sailed towards the Sun, passing Venus about six months into its mission.

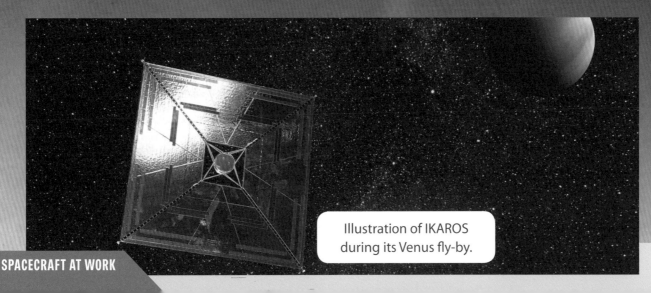

Illustration of IKAROS during its Venus fly-by.

CHAPTER 5
Shuttle-Mir Era

Mir Space Station (left), space shuttle (right)

38 First African American in Space

Guion Bluford Jr. launched to space on August 30, 1983

Even today, minorities, especially African Americans, face racism and stereotyping. When an African American does something that no African American has done before, it is a huge deal.

On August 30, 1983, retired United States Air Force colonel Dr. Guion (Guy) Stewart Bluford Jr. became the first African American in space. His role was that of a mission specialist. Bluford flew on three more space shuttle missions during his career at NASA.

The primary mission of Bluford's first flight (STS-8) was to deploy a weather satellite for India, but the astronauts also performed several dozen experiments to further understand the effects of spaceflight on the human body.

Astronaut Guion Bluford Jr. uses the treadmill aboard the space shuttle.

Although Guion Bluford Jr. was the first African American in space, he was not the first of African descent to go to space. That title goes to a cosmonaut named Arnaldo Tamayo Méndez from Guantánamo, Cuba.

The first African American woman in space was named Mae Carol Jemison. Jemison travelled to space aboard the space shuttle *Endeavour* in 1992.

39 The Shuttle

First space shuttle launched on April 12, 1981

After the success of the Apollo program, people began to believe that humanity's next step would be Mars and beyond! To make this dream a reality, we needed a reusable spacecraft to make space travel routine and inexpensive.

Six space shuttles were constructed, and five of these flew into space — the first in 1981. There were 135 shuttle missions, but it was never routine and it was never cheap. Two of the five space shuttles were lost in horrific disasters, killing 14 astronauts.

Despite the cost, the space shuttle did amazing things. It usually carried 7 astronauts at a time (it once flew with 8). It visited the Russian space station Mir, launched space telescopes like Hubble and Chandra and was used to construct the International Space Station.

This large fuel tank fed liquid oxygen and liquid hydrogen to the three engines on the orbiter.

The *Orbiter* (Shuttle) was 37 metres long, 17 metres high and had a wingspan of almost 24 metres. The cargo bay was over 18 metres long and almost 5 metres wide.

The shuttle used two solid rocket boosters for extra lifting power.

Space shuttle

Space shuttle docked with Mir, photographed from a Soyuz spacecraft.

Sometimes the space shuttle would carry a laboratory, called Spacelab, in its cargo bay. Spacelab was accessible through a tube from the shuttle's main cabin.

The space shuttle landed on a runway just like an airplane. Sometimes it landed in California and would return to Florida atop a modified 747.

The robotic "Canadarm" was designed to lift satellites out of the cargo bay. It could also be used to ferry astronauts around as they worked.

40 Construction in Space

The first space stations were small, lasted only a few months and were fully constructed when launched. The Soviet Union began construction of Mir in space on February 20, 1986. This was the first space station assembled in orbit. Over the next ten years, six pressurized modules were added, as well as scaffolding, solar panels, antennae and other components.

Mir soon became a very diverse place. Before the collapse of the Soviet Union, cosmonauts from Syria, Afghanistan and Bulgaria visited the space station, along with astronauts from France, Japan, the United Kingdom and Austria. Space shuttles visited the space station 10 times as part of the Shuttle–Mir program. The shuttle missions included citizens of Costa Rica, Australia, Peru, Canada and several European nations.

In 1999, cosmonauts left the space station for the last time, and on March 23, 2001, the space station de-orbited, burning up in the atmosphere over the Pacific Ocean.

Mir used a system of cranes, called Strela, as the main tool for construction and repair of the space station.

A busy place in space! This group of astronauts and cosmonauts from the space station and Mir come from six different nations.

Canadian astronaut Chris Hadfield plays guitar aboard Mir.

The Mir Space Station
— the first space station
assembled in orbit.

41 *Challenger* Disaster

Mir construction began on February 20, 1986

A high-school teacher named Christa McAuliffe had trained to become an astronaut. She joined *Challenger*'s crew as part of NASA's new "Teacher in Space" project. Schools around the world tuned in to watch the launch live on television. It was the 25th mission for the space shuttle.

But 73 seconds after lift-off, a seal broke on one of the shuttle's solid rocket boosters. The booster collided with the large external fuel tank and the spacecraft exploded. The seven astronauts were killed. Schools sent their students home for the day, and many employers did the same.

That night, American president Ronald Reagan addressed the world: "We will never forget them, nor the last time we saw them, this morning, as they prepared for their journey and waved goodbye and 'slipped the surly bonds of earth' to 'touch the face of God.'"

Challenger with cargo bay doors open and the Canadarm extended.

The space shuttle exploded on January 28, 1986, in a giant white cloud as the fuel, hydrogen and oxygen, combined to make water.

The crew of STS-51L (*Challenger*'s mission name). Left to right: Ellison S. Onizuka, Michael J. Smith, Sharon Christa McAuliffe, Francis R. (Dick) Scobee, Gregory Jarvis, Ronald E. McNair, Judith A. Resnik.

In 2003, another tragedy struck the shuttle program when the space shuttle *Columbia* broke apart while re-entering Earth's atmosphere. All seven astronauts were lost.

CHAPTER 6
Exploring the Universe

Hubble Space Telescope

42 Hubble Space Telescope

Hubble launched on April 24, 1990

Did you know that only certain types of light make it through Earth's atmosphere? Not only that, the light that does make it down to Earth bounces around. It's like looking at a light from the bottom of a swimming pool. Astronomers have long dreamed of putting a powerful telescope in outer space to get a clearer view.

The Hubble Space Telescope wasn't the first space telescope, but it was by far the most powerful. Hubble's photographs of the cosmos changed the way we see the universe. The telescope not only sees in visible light, but also in infrared (longer wavelengths) and ultra-violet (shorter wavelengths).

Hubble has taken millions of observations, resulting in tens of thousands of publications. Its data has been used to win a **Nobel Prize**!

Hubble Space Telescope

The Hubble Space Telescope is named for astronomer Edwin Hubble, who discovered the expansion of the universe.

This image of the "Pillars of Creation" is one of the Hubble Space Telescope's most famous images.

Blurry vision

Hubble was launched into space on April 24, 1990. When people back on Earth looked at the first image, they realized it was fuzzy. Something was terribly wrong!

Astronauts launched aboard the space shuttle for a repair mission on December 2, 1993. The repair mission lasted over 10 days. The astronauts conducted 5 spacewalks, each lasting about 7 hours. The space shuttle flew 4 additional Hubble servicing missions, the last one in 2009.

The Hubble Space Telescope still operates as of 2020, taking incredible photographs of space, and is expected to continue for many years.

The top image shows a photo of a galaxy before Hubble's repair, and the bottom shows the same galaxy after.

Astronauts make repairs to the Hubble Space Telescope while attached to the Canadarm.

43 Origin of the Universe

COBE launched on November 18, 1989

The universe began with a Big Bang, when matter, energy and time sprang into existence. Based on careful measurements, astronomers have calculated that the Big Bang occurred 13.7 billion years ago. Can we study something that happened so very long ago? The answer is yes! The spacecraft on this page changed the way we see our place in the cosmos.

Light from the early universe can still be seen. This very old light is called the cosmic microwave background, or CMB, and it tells us a lot about the Big Bang and how the universe evolved to form galaxies, stars and planets.

The first spacecraft to study the CMB was called COBE (for Cosmic Background Explorer). Launched in 1989, COBE spent the next four years studying the Big Bang. This research was so groundbreaking that two of COBE's researchers were awarded the Nobel Prize.

COBE launched on November 18, 1989.

Launched on June 30, 2001, this spacecraft, named WMAP, mapped the CMB in high definition, confirming the age of the universe.

This is a map of CMB. Orange shows warmer light and blue shows cooler.

On May 14, 2009, this spacecraft, named Planck, used CMB to measure the amount of **dark matter** in the universe.

44 Finding Exoplanets

Kepler launched on March 7, 2009

Twenty-five years ago, the only planets we knew about were the ones in our Solar System. Then, in 1992, the first extra-solar planets were discovered around another star. We call these new worlds "exoplanets," and the search is on to find a planet with life, just like Earth.

The best way to discover small, rocky planets like Earth is to watch the brightness of a star. If the brightness drops every few days, months or years, there might be a planet (or many planets) around that star. This is called the **Transit Method.**

That's exactly what the Kepler Space Telescope does. From its launch in 2009 to the end of its mission in 2018, Kepler discovered almost 3,000 exoplanets. The data from Kepler can even be used to calculate the size, mass and density of the planet. Once the planet has been found, other telescopes can analyze light passing through the planet's atmosphere to search for signs of life!

Kepler Space Telescope launched on March 7, 2009, and operated until 2018.

This spacecraft, named TESS, launched on April 18, 2018. It is a space telescope that looks at the entire sky, looking for planets around nearby stars.

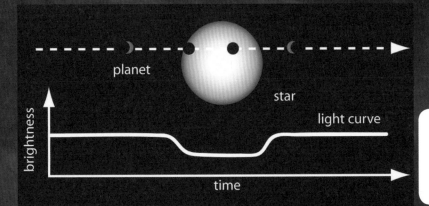

planet

star

light curve

brightness

time

This diagram shows how astronomers use data to measure the dip in a star's brightness to find planets.

45 X-Rays and Black Holes

When we think of X-rays, we usually think of the machines that doctors use to look at our bones. But what are X-rays? X-rays are just light with very high energy. In space, X-rays come from very hot objects. By measuring X-ray energy, researchers can determine what objects are made of, and how fast they are moving.

In 1999, space shuttle *Columbia* carried the Chandra X-Ray Observatory into space. This very special telescope allowed astronomers to study black holes, neutron stars and the centre of galaxies, and is still operational today!

The Chandra Space Telescope helps scientists study black holes — a subject that has fascinated the world for over a century.

Chandra X-Ray Observatory launched on July 23, 1999.

What is a black hole?

At the centre of most galaxies is a black hole. Most black holes are born when a giant star runs out of energy and implodes. A black hole's gravity is so strong that it pulls in anything that gets too close.

An image of a galaxy cluster merger. Hubble Telescope data is blue, while Chandra X-Ray data is shown in pink.

Radiation experts

Did you know that astronomers are radiation experts? Most of the time, when astronomers talk about radiation they are talking about light. Radio, microwaves, gamma rays and X-rays are all just light with different amounts of energy.

Microwaves, like those produced in your microwave oven, and radio waves have much less energy than the light from a lamp. X-rays and gamma rays have much more energy, and can cause damage to the human body.

Everything emits radiation, even you! If you put on a pair of infrared goggles you can see the radiation emitted by your body. This radiation has thousands of times more energy than any cell phone.

A **Van Allen radiation belt** is a zone of charged particles around a planet. The Earth has two Van Allen belts, held in place by its magnetic field.

Astronomers study electromagnetic radiation (in other words, light) of all wavelengths: from radio waves to gamma rays. Everyday light is just a small part of a much larger spectrum.

Cosmic rays

Cosmic rays are particles made up of the cores of atoms. They travel through space at almost the speed of light and may pose a health risk to astronauts on long space flights if their spaceship does not have enough protection.

| Radio waves | Infrared | Ultraviolet | X-rays | Gamma rays |

CHAPTER 7
Ongoing Missions

The International Space Station is made up of different modules.

Dennis Tito launched on April 28, 2001

Have you ever dreamed about going to space, while skipping the years of training required to become an astronaut? On April 28, 2001, a businessman named Dennis Tito paid US$20 million to become the first space tourist! Tito flew to the International Space Station aboard a Russian rocket.

In the 1990s, a space competition called the Ansari X Prize, worth US$10 million, was launched to encourage private companies to invest in spaceflight. To win, the company had to send a spaceship to 100 km in altitude twice in two weeks. The prize was won on June 21, 2004, when SpaceShipOne completed the challenge.

There are several companies in the space tourism business. Most of these spacecraft travel too slowly to enter orbit around the Earth, but still allow the passengers to enjoy several minutes of weightlessness, reach an altitude of at least 100 km and see the curve of the Earth.

BLUE ORIGIN

New Shepard is a spacecraft designed for sub-orbital space tourism.

SpaceShipOne hangs from its flying launch pad, an aircraft called White Knight.

N318SL

47 International Space Station

The International Space Station, or ISS, is the largest, most complex and most expensive project ever to be built in space. The ISS has had such a huge impact, you could write a book of 50 ISS missions that changed the world!

Assembly of the station began in space on November 20, 1998, and the last major modules and components launched in 2011. Missions to the space station are divided into expeditions and last about three months. More than 60 expeditions have been completed so far.

The most important research conducted on the ISS is on the human body. Research is vital for future missions to Mars and beyond, where humans will spend years getting to and from their destinations.

The ISS's *Cupola* module is one of the astronauts' favourite places to hang out. Here, Canadian astronaut Chris Hadfield plays guitar during Expedition 34.

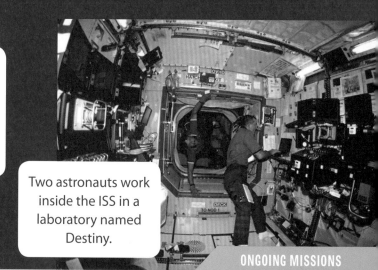

Two astronauts work inside the ISS in a laboratory named Destiny.

A busy place in space

The ISS is a very busy place. During construction, the space shuttle visited the station several times per year. One time, there were 13 people onboard the station! Crewed Russian Soyuz spacecraft also visit the space station about four times per year.

With the space shuttle now retired, uncrewed resupply vessels come and go almost every month. The spacecraft shown on the right are used to supply the ISS with a constant supply of food, experiments and other essential resources.

Progress Resupply Vessel

SpaceX Dragon

Cygnus

Japanese HTV

European Space Agency's (ESA) ATV

Astronauts and cosmonauts aboard a (very cramped) Soyuz spacecraft.

This proton rocket carried *Zarya*, the first module of the International Space Station.

48 Studying Earth's Climate

Terra Satellite launched on December 18, 1999

Climate change is the most important challenge faced by humans today. Climate is defined as the average weather conditions over a long period of time. Thanks in part to Earth-observing spacecraft, researchers have proved that the changing climate is driven by human activities such as cutting down forests and burning fossil fuels.

In the last century, drought and famine have killed far more people than wars and other disasters. Because of global warming, climate disasters are expected to increase. This is why it is so important to study climate change so that solutions can be developed.

This Delta II rocket is about to launch a spacecraft called Orbiting Carbon Observatory-2 on July 2, 2014.

This image of the Earth was created with data from a spacecraft called Terra, which measures Earth's ability to radiate heat into space.

NASA's Aqua Satellite studies the water cycle, creating 3D maps of the Earth's atmosphere. Launched on May 4, 2002.

Japan's GOSAT-2 spacecraft helps researchers separate CO_2 from natural sources and CO_2 emitted by humans. Launched on October 29, 2018.

NASA's Terra Satellite monitors the spread of pollution around the world. Launched on December 18, 1999.

SCISAT is a Canadian spacecraft that studies the atmosphere above the Arctic. Launched on August 13, 2003.

These spacecraft represent only a small sample of a massive fleet of Earth Observation Spacecraft dedicated to climate-change research.

A Swedish spacecraft called Odin uses Canadian instrumentation to study the ozone layer in Earth's atmosphere. Launched on February 20, 2001.

49 Satellite Trains

Until recently, most communication satellites have been placed in **geostationary orbit**, 36,000 km above the equator. That is changing. Each year, thousands of new satellites are orbiting less than 400 km up. Someday soon, if you were to stargaze and count the objects in the sky, these satellites may outnumber the stars!

These new satellites are expected to provide high-speed internet to the entire world. To make this work, thousands of satellites must work together. Often as many as 60 satellites launch together on a single rocket. These satellites form "trains" across the sky before settling into their final orbits. Satellite constellations are expected to become a major nuisance to astronomers.

Image of a satellite train streaking across a mosaic image of the night sky.

This Iridium satellite was part of one of the first satellite constellations. The first launch was on May 5, 1997.

Space junk

There are more than 2,500 satellites orbiting Earth. If some of these spacecraft were to collide, it's possible that so much space junk might be created that humans would no longer have access to space!

50 Reusable Orbital Rockets

It was thought that a reusable rocket — one that could deliver cargo to orbit, return to Earth, be fueled up and fly again — was nearly impossible. Rockets can typically only be used once. They either burn up in the atmosphere or fall into the sea. A company called SpaceX was determined to change this.

SpaceX attempted to land its uncrewed, giant rocket booster on a barge out at sea. It took dozens of attempts, most of which ended in fiery explosions. The first successful landing occurred on December 21, 2015. How will this change the world? Reusable rockets, like reusable airplanes, could open up space-travel to everyone, just as airline travel did a few generations ago.

SpaceX's most impressive first was the first launch of its Falcon Heavy rocket. During this launch, which placed a Tesla Roadster into orbit around the Sun, they landed two of the giant boosters at the same time!

A SpaceX booster after its return to the landing pad. To save cost, SpaceX does not even repaint its rockets between flights.

A Falcon Heavy rocket takes flight, with all three boosters destined to return to Earth to be reused.

The two side boosters return to Earth after launch of a Falcon Heavy rocket.

During the first flight of the Falcon Heavy rocket on February 6, 2018, a mannequin named Starman was placed in a Tesla car, and sent into orbit around the Sun!

The Future

The near future in space is looking very exciting. There are many new and amazing spaceships under construction that will change the way we live, work and do science. NASA and its partners, like Canadian Space Agency and European Space Agency, are even planning to return to the Moon, and soon!

The next generation of super-space telescopes has been constructed, and is almost ready to launch. These telescopes will probe faraway planets for signs of life and look back through time and space to the beginning of the universe.

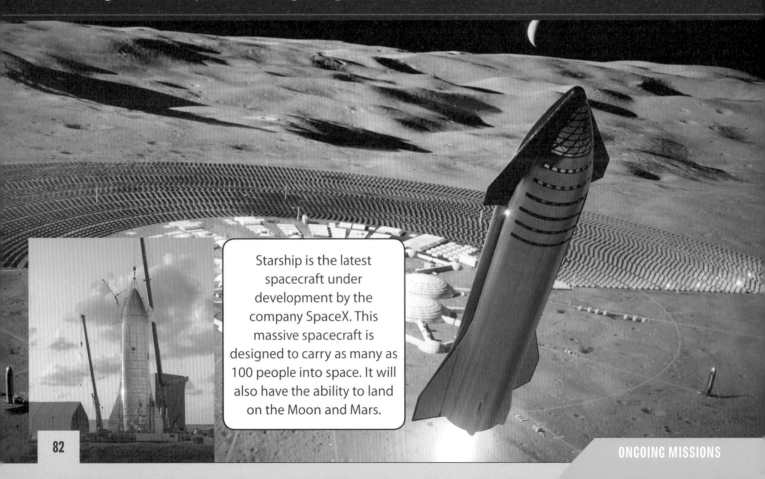

The James Webb Space Telescope (JWST) will be the largest and most complex space telescope ever.

Starship is the latest spacecraft under development by the company SpaceX. This massive spacecraft is designed to carry as many as 100 people into space. It will also have the ability to land on the Moon and Mars.

82

Return to the Moon

The Lunar Gateway is a new space station with assembly beginning in 2022. This outpost will be located near the Moon. It will support crewed missions to the lunar surface and other missions into deep space.

Building the Lunar Gateway will be one of the first uses of NASA's new rocket, the Space Launch System (SLS), and the Orion crewed capsule. This new mission to the Moon has been named Artemis. It aims to land the first woman on the Moon by 2024.

A new lunar lander is in development by the company Blue Origin.

NASA's Space Launch System

In this illustration, an Orion spacecraft approaches the planned Lunar Gateway Space Station.

Glossary

Atmosphere – A layer of air that surrounds a planet.

Atom bomb – A weapon with huge explosive power.

Cold War – Political tension between the United States of America and the Soviet Union between 1947 and 1991.

Communication delay – The time it takes for a signal travelling at the speed of light to reach a spacecraft.

Cosmonaut – A Soviet or Russian astronaut.

Dark matter – A form of matter that is difficult to detect but is believed to account for 85 per cent of the universe.

Electric propulsion – A type of engine that produces thrust by using electricity.

Electromagnetic spectrum – Light at all wavelengths: ranging from low energy radiation like radio waves, microwaves and visible light, to high energy X-rays and gamma rays.

Extra-vehicular activity (EVA) – A spacewalk or lunar expedition where the astronaut is outside of the spacecraft.

Fuel cell – A device that produces electricity and heat by converting hydrogen and oxygen into water.

G force – Short for "gravitational force," a force like gravity, that an astronaut feels while a spacecraft is accelerating or changing direction.

Geostationary orbit – An orbit at the same speed that the Earth is turning, so the satellite seems to stay in a fixed position in the sky.

Geysers – Vents on the surface of a planet that eject high-pressure liquids or gases.

Gravity assist – Using the orbital energy of a planet to either slow down or speed up a spacecraft.

Hydrocarbon – Naturally-occurring molecules made of hydrogen and carbon.

Ion – Atoms (or molecules) with an electrical charge.

Karman Line – An imaginary line between the atmosphere and space (accepted to be 100 km above the surface of the Earth).

Low Earth orbit – An orbit of less than 2,000 km above the Earth. This is where the space station and most satellites reside. Speeds of around 28,000 km/hr must be reached to stay in this orbit, otherwise spacecraft will fall to Earth.

Magnetic field – The magnetic forces generated by a planet or star.

Meteoroid – A small particle from a comet or asteroid orbiting the Sun.

Microgravity – The lack of gravitational pull felt by passengers in an orbiting spacecraft.

NASA – The National Aeronautics and Space Administration, an agency of the United States government.

Nobel Prize – A set of annual international awards in recognition of academic, cultural or scientific advances.

Orbit – The path an object takes around another object, like a spacecraft around a planet, or a planet around a star.

Payload – Passengers or cargo on a vehicle.

Period – The time required to complete one orbit.

Piggybacking – Spacecraft that hitch a ride on a rocket, but are not part of the rocket's primary mission. This is done to save cost.

Radiation – Particles moving outwards from a source. In astronomy, this mainly refers to electromagnetic radiation (i.e., light) at different energy levels, but can also refer to particles moving through magnetic fields.

Remote sensing – In spaceflight, this refers to the process of acquiring information about a moon or planet from orbit.

Retro rockets – Rocket engines designed to slow down a spacecraft for reentry into Earth's atmosphere.

Seismometer – An instrument that responds to ground motions, such as those caused by earthquakes, volcanic eruptions and explosions.

Sounding rocket – A small sub-orbital rocket designed for research. These rockets can reach space but lack the speed to stay in orbit.

Soviet Union – The largest country in the world from 1922 to 1991, at which time the union divided into 15 independent countries, the largest of which is Russia.

Space Race – Competition between the United States of America and Soviet Union to achieve firsts in spaceflight.

Thrust – The force a rocket experiences while the engines are on.

Thrusters – Small rocket engines used to steer a spacecraft.

Telemetry – The transmission of data from a spacecraft.

Trajectory – The path taken by an object in flight.

Van Allen radiation belt – A zone of fast-moving particles held in place by Earth's magnetic field.

Velocity – An object's speed as well as its direction.

Find Out More

There are many air and space museums around the world with excellent websites to help you learn more about space missions. Here are some of the most popular:

North America

Canada Aviation and Space Museum, Ottawa, ON, *ingeniumcanada.org*

Earth Explorer, US Geological Survey, *earthexplorer.usgs.gov*

Smithsonian National Air and Space Museum, Washington, DC, and Chantilly, VA, *airandspace.si.edu*

Kennedy Space Center, FL, *kennedyspacecenter.com*

Space Center Houston, TX, *spacecenter.org*

Europe

National Space Centre, Leicester, United Kingdom, *spacecentre.co.uk*

Musée de l'Air et de l'Espace, Paris, France, *museeairespace.fr*

Technik Museum Speyer, Speyer, Germany, *speyer.technik-museum.de/en*

Other

Memorial Museum of Cosmonautics, Moscow, Russia, *kosmo-museum.ru*

Museum of Applied Arts & Sciences, Powerhouse Museum, Sydney, Australia, *maas.museum/powerhouse-museum*

Photo Credits

PHOTO CREDITS